Contents:

Answers and Mark Schemes

Mathematics Tests 6

English Reading Tests 36

Grammar, Punctuation and Spelling Tests 52

From the founder of Exam Ninja...

Thank you for choosing to buy these Key Stage 2 practice papers by Exam Ninja!

I founded Exam Ninja several years ago with the core purpose of helping children of all ages to do the best they possibly can in their exams. I sincerely hope that this book helps your child achieve their potential in their KS2 SATs.

Exams (like ninjas) are pretty scary things, and so whether it's Key Stage 1, Key Stage 2 or Key Stage 3 SATs tests, Phonics Screening Checks, 11+ exams or GCSEs your child is preparing for, Exam Ninja has the resources they need.

Joshua Geake
Founder and Director of Exam Ninja.

We view exams and tests as an opportunity for your child to show just how talented and special they are. With our resources and a little help and support from you, we can enable them to approach their assessments positively and confidently. We know they can do it!

So from me and everyone at Exam Ninja – good luck for the KS2 SATs in May!

How these tests will help your child

We have devised these Key Stage 2 practice papers to be used at any time throughout the year to provide practice for the Key Stage 2 SATs tests.

As your child works through these tests, they will gain invaluable practice in answering challenging KS2 SATs questions. As our many tens of thousands of customers will tell you: Exam Ninja's resources work! In 2013, 2014 and 2015, over 80% of our customers' children achieved level 5 or more in **all** of their KS2 SATs tests and in 2016, over 80% got a scaled score in excess of 100! Through the use of these practice papers, we believe these results will get even better!

After completing the tests, you will be able to check how well your child has performed and gain a better awareness of their strengths and weaknesses. Once you have identified a weakness, this can be tackled head on with our targeted KS2 SATs packs. See **ExamNinja.co.uk** for more details.

Exam Ninja

© Exam Ninja

Taking the tests

Before your child starts a test, check that everything is prepared for the test to run smoothly:

- Provide a **quiet environment** that's free from distractions such as televisions, smartphones and music players so that children can complete the tests undisturbed.

- Ensure they feel **relaxed and unhurried** when starting the tests. For example, don't start a test just before bedtime or before their favourite television programme!

- They will need the following equipment for the **English Reading and Grammar, Punctuation and Spelling papers**: a pen, pencil and a rubber. **For the Maths tests they will need**: a pen, pencil, rubber, ruler and protractor (angle measurer).

- The amount of time given for each test **varies**, so always check the first page of the paper before your child starts.

- Check your child has asked all the questions they need to ask about the test **before** it begins.

- As part of this book we have provided the audio for the **Spelling Papers** as a **FREE** download. We highly recommend that you use it to provide a very realistic KS2 SATs exam environment.

Be strict about the amount of time you allocate to your child when they take these tests and ensure that they don't leave their seat or ask any questions once a test has begun.

Marking the tests

Once your child has completed a test you can mark it by using the included **Answers and Mark Schemes** booklet. Exam markers do try to award pupils as many marks as they can but they rarely give them the benefit of the doubt, so ensure that you mark their papers **honestly** and **without any bias**.

Within each **Answers and Mark Scheme** section you will find a table to fill in with your child's marks. Take the time to fill these in to keep a record of how they're performing.

Levels and Scaled Scores

Pupils used to be awarded a 'level', such as '3b' or '4c', however for 2016, levels were replaced with 'scaled scores'. **Scaled scores** are simply a different way of reporting your child's exam marks. Instead of being given their marks and a level, their marks will be converted into a scaled score.

Children whose scaled score is close to 100 are judged to have reached the national standard that's expected of them. Those scoring over 100 will have performed above that standard, whilst those that score below 100 have not reached the expected standard.

KEY STAGE 2
MATHEMATICS TESTS

ANSWERS & MARK SCHEMES

© Exam Ninja

About the KS2 Maths Practice Papers

There are three **full** sets of **KS2 Maths Practice Papers**. Each set of KS2 Maths Practice Papers consists of three separate papers: **Paper 1 (Arithmetic), Paper 2 (Reasoning) and Paper 3 (Reasoning)**. Calculators are **strictly not allowed** for **any** of these tests.

 This pencil sign means that an answer needs to be written either where indicated by the pencil or in the position instructed in the question.

Some questions will have an answer box that says "Show your working". Children should use this space to write out their working and their final answer in the smaller box within it. This way, even if a child ultimately gets the answer wrong, they could still be awarded marks for approaching it in the right way.

Paper 1 (Arithmetic)

Paper 1 lasts for **30 minutes** and is out of a total of **40 marks**.

Paper 2 (Reasoning) and Paper 3 (Reasoning)

Paper 2 and Paper 3 each last for **40 minutes** and have a total of **35 marks** each.

Marking and Assessing

Once your child has completed a test, mark it using the **Answers and Mark Schemes** within this book, add up the marks and enter them in the table below. After completing a full set of papers, add up the scores for Paper 1, Paper 2 and the Paper 3 to get a total out of **110**.

Maths Marks Table

	SET A	SET B	SET C
Paper 1 (30 mins, out of 40)			
Paper 2 (40 mins, out of 35)			
Paper 3 (40 mins, out of 35)			
Total (out of 110)			

Mathematics - Paper 1 (Arithmetic) Set A Answers

Q	Mark	Answers
1.	1	1,143
2.	1	1,410
3.	1	301
4.	1	301
5.	1	1,241
6.	1	23
7.	1	509
8.	1	1,966
9.	1	58
10.	1	55,725
11.	1	170
12.	1	200,000
13.	1	344
14.	1	100
15.	1	9.387
16.	1	7.86
17.	1	30
18.	1	72

Exam Ninja

© Exam Ninja

Q	Mark	Answers
19.	1	$\frac{9}{25}$ *Accept an equivalent fraction or decimal such as $\frac{18}{50}$ or 0.36.*
20.	1	37.778
21.	1	112
22.	1	779.46
23.	Up to 2	4,806 *Award **2 marks** for the correct answer.* *Incorrect answer? Award **1 mark** for a correct method which contains no more than **one** arithmetic error.* ***Do not** award a mark if the error is in the place value.* ***Do not** award a mark if the final answer is missing.*
24.	1	102
25.	1	93,404
26.	1	$\frac{7}{20}$ *Accept an equivalent fraction or decimal such as $\frac{35}{100}$ or 0.35*
27.	1	16
28.	1	0.025
29.	Up to 2	19,685 *Award **2 marks** for the correct answer.* *Incorrect answer? Award **1 mark** for a correct method which contains no more than **one** arithmetic error.* ***Do not** award a mark if the error is in the place value.* ***Do not** award a mark if the final answer is missing.*
30.	1	$1\frac{1}{5}$ *Accept an equivalent fraction or decimal such as $\frac{6}{5}$ or 1.2*
31.	1	36

Q	Mark	Answers
32.	1	$2\frac{7}{30}$ Accept an equivalent fraction or decimal such as $1\frac{37}{30}$ or $2.2\dot{3}$. **Do not** award a mark if the decimal is rounded or truncated. There must be evidence that the digit 3 recurs.
33.	1	$\frac{11}{12}$ Accept an equivalent fraction or decimal such as $\frac{22}{24}$ or $0.91\dot{6}$. **Do not** award a mark if the decimal is rounded or truncated. There must be evidence that the digit 6 is a recurring digit.
34.	Up to 2	29 Award **2 marks** for the correct answer. Incorrect answer? Award **1 mark** for a correct method which contains no more than **one** arithmetic error. Award **1 mark** for a correct short-division method only if there is evidence of carrying figures. **Do not** award a mark if the final answer is missing.
35.	1	65
36.	Up to 2	203 Award **2 marks** for the correct answer. Incorrect answer? Award **1 mark** for a correct method which contains no more than **one** arithmetic error. Award **1 mark** for a correct short-division method only if there is evidence of carrying figures. **Do not** award a mark if the final answer is missing.

Exam Ninja

© Exam Ninja

Mathematics - Paper 1 (Arithmetic) Set B Answers

Q	Mark	Answers	Exam Ninja	Page 11 of 84
1.	1	206		
2.	1	414		
3.	1	657		
4.	1	0.01		
5.	1	12,294		
6.	1	274		
7.	1	13		
8.	1	132		
9.	1	496		
10.	1	616		
11.	1	846		
12.	1	509		
13.	1	32.249		
14.	1	4,500		
15.	1	2,080		
16.	1	15.314		
17.	1	15		
18.	1	50,500		

Q	Mark	Answers
19.	1	$1\frac{12}{25}$ Accept an equivalent fraction or decimal such as $\frac{37}{25}$ or 1.48.
20.	1	190,468
21.	1	66.55
22.	1	800.2
23.	Up to 2	1,645 Award **2 marks** for the correct answer. Incorrect answer? Award **1 mark** for a correct method which contains no more than **one** arithmetic error. **Do not** award a mark if the error is in the place value. **Do not** award a mark if the final answer is missing.
24.	1	0.05 or $\frac{1}{20}$
25.	1	91
26.	1	$4\frac{7}{24}$ Accept an equivalent fraction or decimal such as $4\frac{14}{48}$ or $4.291\dot{6}$. **Do not** award a mark if the decimal is rounded or truncated. There must be evidence that the digit 6 recurs.
27.	Up to 2	45 Award **2 marks** for the correct answer. Incorrect answer? Award **1 mark** for a correct method which contains no more than **one** arithmetic error. **Do not** award a mark if the error is in the place value. **Do not** award a mark if the final answer is missing.
28.	1	156

Exam.Ninja

© Exam Ninja

Q	Mark	Answers
29.	Up to 2	31,552 Award **2 marks** for the correct answer. Incorrect answer? Award **1 mark** for a correct method which contains no more than **one** arithmetic error. **Do not** award a mark if the error is in the place value. **Do not** award a mark if the final answer is missing.
30.	1	$3\frac{1}{7}$ Accept an equivalent fraction or decimal such as $\frac{22}{7}$ or 3.1428571. **Do not** award a mark if the decimal is rounded or truncated.
31.	1	$\frac{11}{15}$ Accept an equivalent fraction or decimal such as $\frac{22}{30}$ or $0.7\dot{3}$. **Do not** award a mark if the decimal is rounded or truncated. There must be evidence that the digit 3 recurs.
32.	1	200
33.	1	73
34.	Up to 2	323 Award **2 marks** for the correct answer. Incorrect answer? Award **1 mark** for a correct method which contains no more than **one** arithmetic error. Award **1 mark** for a correct short-division method only if there is evidence of carrying figures. **Do not** award a mark if the final answer is missing.
35.	1	100
36.	1	$5\frac{19}{20}$ Accept an equivalent fraction or decimal such as $\frac{119}{20}$ or 5.95. **Do not** award a mark if the decimal is rounded or truncated.

Mathematics - Paper 1 (Arithmetic) Set C Answers

Q	Mark	Answers
1.	1	22
2.	1	454
3.	1	1,134
4.	1	391
5.	1	40,791
6.	1	36,000
7.	1	5.2
8.	1	490
9.	1	1,498
10.	1	165
11.	1	72
12.	1	235
13.	1	1,800
14.	1	1
15.	1	57
16.	1	100
17.	1	28
18.	1	39.114

Exam Ninja

© Exam Ninja

Q	Mark	Answers
19.	1	$1\dfrac{9}{20}$ *Accept an equivalent fraction or decimal such as* $\dfrac{29}{20}$ *or 1.45.*
20.	1	13.2
21.	1	999,996
22.	1	101.58
23.	Up to 2	9,506 *Award **2 marks** for the correct answer.* *Incorrect answer? Award **1 mark** for a correct method which contains no more than **one** arithmetic error.* ***Do not** award a mark if the error is in the place value.* ***Do not** award a mark if the final answer is missing.*
24.	1	0.00002
25.	1	4,349.25
26.	1	180
27.	Up to 2	244 *Award **2 marks** for the correct answer.* *Incorrect answer? Award **1 mark** for a correct method which contains no more than **one** arithmetic error.* *Award **1 mark** for a correct short-division method only if there is evidence of carrying figures.* ***Do not** award a mark if the final answer is missing.*
28.	1	$\dfrac{1}{9}$ *Accept an equivalent fraction or decimal such as* $\dfrac{2}{18}$ *or 0.1.* *There must be evidence that the digit 1 recurs.*

Q	Mark	Answers
29.	Up to 2	19,980 Award **2 marks** for the correct answer. Incorrect answer? Award **1 mark** for a correct method which contains no more than **one** arithmetic error. **Do not** award a mark if the error is in the place value. **Do not** award a mark if the final answer is missing.
30.	1	112
31.	1	0.81
32.	1	2
33.	1	$1\frac{1}{8}$ Accept an equivalent fraction or decimal such as $\frac{9}{8}$ or 1.125. **Do not** award a mark if the decimal is rounded or truncated.
34.	Up to 2	304 Award **2 marks** for the correct answer. Incorrect answer? Award **1 mark** for a correct method which contains no more than **one** arithmetic error. Award **1 mark** for a correct short-division method only if there is evidence of carrying figures. **Do not** award a mark if the final answer is missing.
35.	1	54
36.	1	3

Exam.Ninja

© Exam Ninja

Mathematics - Paper 2 (Reasoning) Set A Answers

Q	Mark	Answers
1.	1	160 , 640 *Award **1 mark** to pupils that correctly circle **both** answers.*
2.	Up to 2	$8 + 9 = 17$ $6 \times 7 = 42$ $17 - 6 = 11$ $10 \div 5 = 2$ *Award **2 marks** for **four** correct sums.* *Incorrect answer? Award **1 mark** for **two** correct sums.*
3.	Up to 2	2:11pm 19 minutes *Award **1 mark** for **each** correct answer.*
4.	1	
5.	1 1 1	40 children. 15 fewer children. *What's unusual is that see saws normally require an **even** number of people to use them. The pictogram suggests 25 children used the see saw which is an **odd** number.*
6.	1	40, 80
7.	1	Circle, Square, Rectangle and Triangle.
8.	Up to 2	£0.10 *Award **2 marks** for the correct answer.* *Incorrect answer? Award **1 mark** to pupils whose working shows that the paper cost £2.10.*

Q	Mark	Answers
9.	1	35kg
	1	(scale diagram showing pointer at approximately 30, scale marked 0 10 20 30 40 50, labelled kg)
10.	1	7 8 8 7
11.	1	537
12.	1	0.25, $\dfrac{1}{3}$, 0.45, $\dfrac{3}{5}$
13.	1	140cm
	Up to 2	700cm^2 Award **2 marks** for the correct answer. Incorrect answer? Award **1 mark** if there's evidence of a suitable method. E.g. Adding up the grid boxes or calculating and adding up the individual areas of the square and the rectangle.
14.	Up to 2	$\begin{array}{r} 6\ 4\ \boxed{8} \\ +\ \boxed{2}\ 6\ 9 \\ \hline 9\ \boxed{1}\ 7 \end{array}$ Award **2 marks** for the correct answer. Incorrect answer? Award **1 mark** if there's **two** correct digits.
15.	1	2
16.	Up to 2	£7.20 Award **2 marks** for the correct answer. Incorrect answer? Award **1 mark** to pupils whose working shows that 600g = 150g x 4 or that the answer can be found by multiplying £1.80 by 4 or by repeated addition.
17.	1	100
	1	10
	1	9

Exam Ninja

© Exam Ninja

Q	Mark	Answers
18.	Up to 2	120 Award **2 marks** for the correct answer. Incorrect answer? Award **1 mark** to pupils whose working shows that 5% of the number is 8 or a multiple of 8 (for example 10% = 16 etc).
19.	1 1	C = (15,25) 200cm²
20.	Up to 2	n = 4 Award **2 marks** for the correct answer. Incorrect answer? Award **1 mark** to pupils whose working shows that 5n = 20.

Mathematics - Paper 2 (Reasoning) Set B Answers

Q	Mark	Answers
1.	1	0.25, $\frac{1}{4}$ *Award **1 mark** only if **both** answers are correctly circled.*
2.	1	140°
3.	1 Up to 2	£10.50 £8.45 *Award **2 marks** for the correct answer. Incorrect answer? Award **1 mark** to pupils whose working shows that the service charge is £1.05*
4.	1	35, 83
5.	Up to 2	9 × 8 – 42 = 30 *Award **2 marks** for the correct answer.*
6.	1 1	25km 5km
7.	1 1	44,961 10,064
8.	1 1	7:55a.m. 9:03a.m.
9.	1	3,140mm
10.	1 Up to 2	10 baguettes 28 teaspoons *Award **2 marks** for the correct answer* *Incorrect answer? Award **1 mark** to pupils whose working shows that 20 teaspoons of mustard were used in the morning **or** that 8 teaspoons of mustard were used in the afternoon.*
11.	1 Up to 2	20% 40 *Award **2 marks** for the correct answer. Incorrect answer? Award **1 mark** to pupils whose working shows that the angle between Beef and Mustard is 36°.*

Exam.Ninja

© Exam Ninja

Q	Mark	Answers
12.	Up to 2	

×	6	7	8
2	12	14	16
3	18	21	24
4	24	28	32

Award **2 marks** for a fully correct grid.

Incorrect answer? Award **1 mark** for **four** correctly answered multiplications.

Q	Mark	Answers
13.	1	5 coins
	1	146 coins
14.	1	24cm
	Up to 2	$23cm^2$

Award **2 marks** for the correct answer.

Incorrect answer? Award **1 mark** to pupils whose working clearly shows that the total area can be split up into a number of smaller areas and added up.

15. Up to 2

Award **2 marks** for a correctly answered number machine.

Incorrect answer? **Award 1** mark for **two** correctly answered boxes within the number machine.

16. 1

MIRROR LINE

Q	Mark	Answers
17.	Up to 2	0.8 $\boxed{<}$ 1 $\boxed{=}$ 1.0 $\frac{3}{4}$ $\boxed{=}$ $\frac{6}{8}$ $\boxed{<}$ $\frac{8}{6}$ 55% $\boxed{>}$ $\frac{1}{2}$ $\boxed{>}$ 0.45 0.45 $\boxed{<}$ $\frac{4}{5}$ $\boxed{>}$ 0.55 *Award **2 marks** if **all** of the boxes are correctly answered.* *Incorrect answer? Award **1 mark** for **two** entirely correct rows.*
18.	Up to 2	 *Award **2 marks** if **all** of the numbers are correctly placed.* *Incorrect answer? Award **1 mark** for **three** correctly placed numbers.*

Exam Ninja

© Exam Ninja

Mathematics - Paper 2 (Reasoning) Set C Answers

Q	Mark	Answers
1.	1	725,000 is less than ¾ million because ¾ million is 750,000.
2.	1	60, 66, 36, 24
3.	1 1	5 27
4.	1 1	Three pounds and forty five pence (accept three pounds forty five). 3x £1 coins, 2x 20p coins, 1x5p coin or another combination of five coins that total £3.45.
5.	1 1	36 biscuits £11.40
6.	1	Pupils need to shade any **two** tiles on the grid. For example:
7.	1 1	2 hours and 2 minutes. 11:05a.m. (accept answers that simply state 11:05)
8.	1	25, 12.5 Award **1 mark** to pupils who circle **both** numbers. **Do not** award the mark if any other number is circled.
9.	1	C = (7 , 3)
10.	Up to 2	8m Award **2 marks** for the correct answer. Incorrect answer? Award **1 mark** to pupils whose working shows that the total width of the row of buildings is 48m.
11.	Up to 2	Coffee = £1.00, Tea = £0.80 Award **2 marks** for the correct answer. Incorrect answer? Award **1 mark** to pupils with one correct answer for either coffee **or** tea.

Q	Mark	Answers

12. | Up to 2 |

Cuboid

Pyramid

Cube

Incorrect answer? Award **1 mark** *to pupils that have correctly drawn* **three** *links.*

Award **2 marks** *for the correct answer.*

13. | Up to 2 | 2,200

Award **2 marks** *for the correct answer.*

Incorrect answer? Award **1 mark** *to pupils whose working shows that each box can contain up to 440 screws.*

14. | Up to 2 |

Multiples of 8   Multiples of 6

8, 56, 16   48

2   68

Award **2 marks** *for a correctly completed Venn diagram.*

Incorrect answer? Award **1 mark** *to pupils that have correctly placed* **four** *numbers.*

15. | Up to 2 | 70kg

Award **2 marks** *for the correct answer.*

Incorrect answer? Award **1 mark** *to pupils whose working clearly shows Emily's weight as being 35kg.*

16. | Up to 2 |

A —————— 55cl

B   7.5l

C   9,500ml

D   6 ½ l

Award **2 marks** *if* **all** *the capacities are correctly linked.*

Incorrect answer? Award **1 mark** *to pupils that correctly link two capacities.*

17. | Up to 2 | 729cm^3

Award **2 marks** *for the correct answer.*

Incorrect answer? Award **1 mark** *to pupils whose working shows that the volume of a single cube is 27cm^3.*

Exam Ninja

© Exam Ninja

Q	Mark	Answers
18.	1	
19.	Up to 2	50% [<] $\frac{18}{24}$ [<] 0.9 $\frac{1}{4}$ [<] 33% [>] $\frac{1}{4}$ 25% [=] $\frac{1}{4}$ [=] 0.25 $\frac{25}{50}$ [>] 25% [=] 0.25 *Award **2 marks** if **all** the boxes are correctly answered.* *Incorrect answer? Award **1 mark** for **two** entirely correct rows. Note that the **entire row** must be correctly answered.*
20.	Up to 2	£18.12 *Award **2 marks** for the correct answer.* *Incorrect answer? Award **1 mark** to pupils whose working clearly shows that the total amount collected is £36.24.*
21.	1	

Mathematics - Paper 3 (Reasoning) Set A Answers

Q	Mark	Answers
1.	1	$249 \frac{3}{5}$
2.	Up to 2	£5.50 Award **2 marks** for the correct answer. Incorrect answer? Award **1 mark** to pupils whose working clearly shows that they have attempted to divide 605 by 110.
3.	1	63 + **50** = 113 7 × **13** = 91
4.	1	$39 \frac{1}{2}$ minutes (accept 39.5 minutes or 39 minutes and 30 seconds)
5.	1	15°C
6.	1	DXXXIV
7.	1	Emily is wrong because the number 14 has **four** factors : 1, 2, 7 and 14.
8.	Up to 2	576 cars Award **2 marks** for the correct answer. Incorrect answer? Award **1 mark** to pupils whose method includes no more than one arithmetic error.
	1	288 cars
9.	1	29th March
	1	Tuesday
10.	1	
	1	

Exam.Ninja © Exam Ninja

Q	Mark	Answers

11. | 1 |

Time	9am	10am	11am	12pm	1pm	2pm
Cars	40	20	10	20	30	20

| | 1 | 140 cars |
| | 1 | 11a.m. |

12. | 1 |

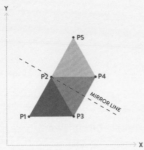

| | **Up to 2** | *Award **1 mark** for a correctly placed mirror line.*
P4 = (4,3) ,P5 = (3,5)
*Award **1 mark** for **each** correct answer.* |

13. | **Up to 2** |

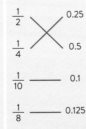

$\frac{1}{2}$ — 0.25
$\frac{1}{4}$ — 0.5
$\frac{1}{10}$ — 0.1
$\frac{1}{8}$ — 0.125

*Award **2 marks** for the correct answer.*
*Incorrect answer? Award **1 mark** if there are **two** correct links.*

14. | 1 | **38** × 3 = 114 |

15. | 1 |

$$\boxed{6} + \boxed{4} = \boxed{10}$$

$$\boxed{2} \times \boxed{9} = \boxed{18}$$

16. | 1 | 68m |
| | 1 | 288m² |
| | 1 | 50% |

Q	Mark	Answers
17.	Up to 2	£0.39 or 39p *Award **2 marks** for the correct answer.* *Incorrect answer? Award **1 mark** to pupils whose working shows that the 3 drinks cost £1.17.*
18.	1 Up to 2	18 families 153l *Award **2 marks** for the correct answer.* *Incorrect answer? Award **1 mark** to pupils whose working shows they have attempted to multiply each row and add together the results.*
19.	Up to 2	300cm 500g 300ml *Award **2 marks** for correctly circling every answer.* *Incorrect answer? Award **1 mark** to pupils that correctly circle **two** answers.*

Exam Ninja

© Exam Ninja

Mathematics - Paper 3 (Reasoning) Set B Answers

Q	Mark	Answers
1.	1	5.75, 6.0
2.	Up to 2	 Award **2 marks** for a correctly labelled pie chart. Incorrect answer? Award **1 mark** if there are **two** correctly labelled segments of the pie chart.
3.	1 1	20% 10.25l or $10\frac{1}{4}$ l
4.	1 1	$6 + 3 = 3 \times 3$ $18 \div 9 = 7 - 5$
5.	1	24.66
6.	1 1	55cm 45cm
7.	Up to 2	£12.10 Award **2 marks** for the correct answer. Incorrect answer? Award **1 mark** to pupils whose working shows they have attempted to sum three burgers, one pizza and a salad.
	1	£13.31
	Up to 2	£6.69 Award **2 marks** for the correct answer. Incorrect answer? Award **1 mark** to pupils whose working indicates that they have attempted to subtract the previous answer from £20.00.

Q	Mark	Answers
8.	1 1	07:25 09:55
9.	1	100g, 1,000g, 10kg, 10 tonnes
10.	1	7.75 (Accept $7\frac{3}{4}$).
11.	Up to 2	130° Award **2 marks** for the correct answer. Incorrect answer? Award **1 mark** to pupils whose working shows that they have attempted to sum two/three angles and subtract them from 270/360.
12.	1	$\frac{3}{8}$ of the shape is shaded (accept $\frac{6}{16}$)
13.	Up to 2	 Award **1 mark** for **each** correct answer.
14.	Up to 2	Sofa A = 270cm Sofa B = 180cm Award **2 marks** for the correct answer. Incorrect answer? Award **1 mark** to pupils whose working clearly shows that 2x(Sofa B) + 90 = 450cm.
15.	1	3 6 > 3 2 6 4 < 7 6 2 9 > 2 5
16.	1	C = (30,15)

Exam Ninja

© Exam Ninja

Q	Mark	Answers
17.	1 Up to 2	80cm 175cm^2 Award **2 marks** for the correct answer. Incorrect answer? Award **1 mark** to pupils whose working shows that each tile within the grid has an area of 25cm^2.
18.	1	5
19.	Up to 2	No, 48 has 10 factors (1, 2, 3, 4, 6, 8, 12, 16, 24 and 48). Award **2 marks** to pupils that have stated 'No' and gone on to list **all** the factors. Incorrect answer? Award **1 mark** to pupils that have answered 'No' and listed some but not all its factors.
20.	1	5 times

Mathematics - Paper 3 (Reasoning) Set C Answers

Q	Mark	Answers
1.	1	35kg
2.	1	6cm
3.	1	6.06, 6.4, $6\frac{1}{2}$, 6.55, 6.60
4.	Up to 2	$\frac{1}{7}$ $\frac{3}{12}$ (or $\frac{1}{4}$ if the pupil's chosen to simplify the fraction to its lowest form) $\frac{2}{8}$ (or $\frac{1}{4}$ if the pupil's chosen to simplify the fraction to its lowest form) Award **2 marks** for answering **all** the questions correctly. Incorrect answer? Award pupils **1 mark** if they have correctly answered **two** questions.
5.	1 1	7 DVDs £0.55 (accept 55p)
6.	1 1	11 hours 36 hours
7.	1	3.75
8.	1 1	5 teas 30 teas
9.	1	30cm
10.	Up to 2	$\frac{18}{10}$ [<] 2.0 [<] 18 3.6 [>] $\frac{14}{7}$ [<] 6.3 Award **2 marks** if **all** the boxes are correctly answered. Incorrect answer? Award **1 mark** for one entirely correct row. Note that the **entire row** must be correctly answered.

Exam Ninja

© Exam Ninja

Q	Mark	Answers
11.	1 1	15mm 3p.m.
12.	Up to 2	£3.75 *Award **2 marks** for the correct answer.* *Incorrect answer? Award **1 mark** to pupils whose working clearly shows that £7.50 was spent at the cinema.*
13.	Up to 2	Faces: **5** Edges: **8** Vertices: **5** Faces: **6** Edges: **12** Vertices: **8** *Award **2 marks** for the correct answer.* *Incorrect answer? Award **1 mark** to pupils that have correctly completed the details for an entire shape.*
14.	1 1	3rd July Monday
15.	Up to 2	750m² *Award **2 marks** for the correct answer.* *Incorrect answer? Award **1 mark** to pupils whose working clearly shows that the horizontal length of two playing fields is 100m or that each playing field has dimensions of 15m x 50m.*
16.	1	**110°** *Award **1 mark** for an illustration with an angle that correctly measures 110°. Use a protractor to ensure it has been correctly drawn. **Do not** award the mark if the pupil has not used a ruler. Accept an accuracy of ±2°.*

17. | **1**

$\frac{1}{4}$ — 0.166

$\frac{2}{3}$ — 0.25

$\frac{1}{6}$ — 0.66

$\frac{1}{5}$ —— 0.2

(lines cross: $\frac{1}{4}$ → 0.25, $\frac{2}{3}$ → 0.66, $\frac{1}{6}$ → 0.166, $\frac{1}{5}$ → 0.2)

18. | **Up to 2**

Award **2 marks** for pupils that correctly draw **all** the mirror lines for all **three** shapes.

Incorrect answer? Award **1 mark** to pupils that correctly draw the mirror lines for **two** shapes.

19. | **Up to 2**

$\frac{2}{5} + \boxed{\frac{4}{10}} = \frac{4}{5}$

$\frac{2}{5} \times \boxed{\frac{10}{5}} = \frac{4}{5}$

Award **2 marks** for pupils that answer the question correctly.

20. | **Up to 2**

Multiples of 8   Multiples of 6

4

40   24   12
       48   18
             36

Award **2 marks** for a correctly completed Venn diagram.

Incorrect answer? Award **1 mark** to pupils that have correctly placed **five** numbers.

21. | **Up to 2**

2 tonnes

250ml

100m

Award **2 marks** for correctly circling every answer.

Incorrect answer? Award **1 mark** to pupils that correctly circle **two** answers.

Exam Ninja

© Exam Ninja

BLANK PAGE

KEY STAGE 2
ENGLISH READING

ANSWERS & MARK SCHEMES

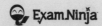

© Exam Ninja

About the KS2 English Reading Practice Papers

There are three full sets of **KS2 English Reading Papers**.

Each set of KS2 English Reading Practice Papers consists of two separate booklets: a **Reading Booklet** and a **Reading Answer Booklet**.

Children are given a total of **60 minutes** to read the **three texts** within the Reading Booklet and use that information to answer all the questions within the Reading Answer Booklet. There are a maximum of **50 marks** available.

 This pencil sign means that an answer needs to be written either where indicated by the pencil or in the position instructed in the question.

Marking and Assessing the Papers

Once your child has completed a test, mark it using the **Answers and Mark Scheme** within this book, add up the marks to get a total out of **50** and enter them in the table below.

English Reading Marks Table

	SET A	SET B	SET C
Reading Answer Booklet (60 mins, out of 50)			

English Reading - Set A - Hurricanes

Q	Mark	Answers
1.	**Up to 2**	Hurricane — Northeast Pacific Typhoon — Northwest Pacific Cyclone — South Pacific *Award **2 marks** for correctly linking **all three**.* *Incorrect answer? Award **1 mark** if the pupil has drawn **one** correct link.*
2.	1	*Award **1 mark** to pupils that explain 'sustained' as meaning 'constant', 'continuous' or 'continuing without interruption' or simply that it stays the same for a period of time (accept a similar explanation).*
3.	1	*The **second** option:* Hurricanes are more powerful over land than at sea.
4.	1	*Award **1 mark** to pupils who state that the area around the eye has the strongest winds or simply strong winds (accept a similar explanation).*
5.	**Up to 2**	*Award **2 marks** if the answer indicates that it's because coastal regions are closest to the sea **and** that this is where hurricanes are formed.* *Award **1 mark** to pupils whose answers only state **one** of the above.*
6.	1	*The **second** option:* When its wind speed is faster than 63 km per hour.
7.	**Up to 2**	• Tornadoes • High Waves • Widespread Flooding • Violent Wind • Heavy Rain *Award **2 marks** to pupils who correctly state **any three** of the above.* *Incorrect answer? Award **1 mark** to pupils that state **any two** of the above.*
8.	1	*Award **1 mark** if the answer indicates that by using sub-headings, the author is trying to make the information easier or faster to read (accept a similar explanation).*
9.	1	*Award **1 mark** if the answer indicates that the author uses the word 'violent' to convey that hurricanes are very destructive and can kill people (accept a similar explanation).*
10.	1	*The **third** option:* Hurricanes are extremely hot.

Exam.Ninja

© Exam Ninja

Q	Mark	Answers
11.	Up to 2	Award **2 marks** to pupils who state that 'Hurricanes' is written to help readers **understand hurricanes** and that it is a **factual** text. For the full **2 marks**, pupils also **need** to quote **two** examples from the text. Examples: • A hurricane is an immense tropical storm. • A hurricane can release as much as 9 trillion litres of rain a day! • A tropical depression becomes a tropical storm, and is given a name, when its sustained wind speeds top 63 km per hour. • Coastal regions are most at danger from hurricanes. • In 2005, Hurricane Katrina killed over 1,800 people.

English Reading - Set A - A Day Out Flying

Q	Mark	Answers
12.	1	Pleasure flights.
13.	Up to 2	Award **2 marks** if the answer suggests pleasure flights are for fun rather than transport **and** go on to explain that you come back to the same place that you started.
14.	1	A raffle at the school fete.
15.	1	A pilot.
16.	1	Award **1 mark** if the answer suggests that Georgina and John like, or are excited by or are interested in planes (accept a similar explanation).
17.	1	The **third** option: An EC120, max speed 150km, endurance of 4hrs 56mins and five seats.
18.	1	Award **1 mark** to pupils who state it's because someone was needed to watch or take care of the dog (accept a similar explanation). **Do not** award the mark to pupils that simply state 'the dog'.
19.	1	Accelerated.
20.	1	Once the plane levelled out.
21.	1	The **third** option: He was anxious.

Q	Mark	Answers
22.	1	*The second option:* Because Frank wanted to show the children a better view.
23.	1	• School • Park • Yellow Fields • M20 • Towns • Countryside • Leeds Castle *Award 1 mark for listing any three of the above.*
24.	1	*The third option:* Robert de Crevecoeur in 1119 as a Norman stronghold.
25.	Up to 2	*Award 2 marks to pupils who explain that by writing 'A Day Out Flying' in the third person, it allows the author to explain different points of view. For the full 2 marks, pupils also need to quote two examples from the text.* Examples: • They guessed their dad was scared of flying. • He looked a little worried. • "Brilliant!" exclaimed John. • "Amazing," grinned Georgina.

English Reading - Set A - Jim's Tree House

Q	Mark	Answers
26.	1	*The second option:* A manual.
27.	1	Sketching.
28.	1	*Award 1 mark if the answer indicates that Jim wanted to build a bridge between the oak tree and the apple tree.*
29.	1	*Award 1 mark if the answer indicates that Jim's mother was concerned that the tree house would harm or damage the tree (accept a similar explanation).*

Exam Ninja

© Exam Ninja

Q	Mark	Answers
30.	1	*Award **1 mark** to pupils who explain that '**pondered**' means thought about, considered or contemplated (accept a similar explanation).*
31.	1	*Award **1 mark** if the pupil's answer states that Jim's eyes were wide **and** his mouth dropped open.*
32.	1	It was boring.
33.	1	*The **second** option:* Shocked and annoyed.
34.	1	Jim would have the benefit of both designs.
35.	1	Amend.
36.	Up to 2	*Award **2 marks** to pupils who correctly identify that Jim's pod would only be large enough for one person **and** that an adult would be unable to climb the rope.* *Award **1 mark** to pupils who correctly identify **one** of the reasons above.*
37.	1	*Award **1 mark** if the answer indicates that Jim was not sure whether he would be able to find the chains to build a chain bridge and so kept the rope bridge design just in case.*
38.	1	*Award **1 mark** if the answer indicates that '**properly equipped**' means to be ready with all the right tools, materials or equipment (accept a similar explanation).*
39.	1	*Award **1 mark** if the answer mentions either inverted commas or speech marks. Accept mentions of an exclamation mark if it also includes the mention of inverted commas or speech marks.*
40.	1	*Award **1 mark** to pupils who suggest Jim felt excited (accept a similar explanation) **and** go on to quote the example '**Squealed in delight**'.*

Q	Mark	Answers
41.	1	*Award **1 mark** to pupils who suggest Jim's parents liked the idea. This is evidenced by them helping him to think about the design, collect materials and tools and to build it. Pupils also need to quote an example from the text to support this.* Examples: • It was even better than before and he was glad he'd spoken to his mum. • For months they had been collecting bits of wood and rope from the industrial estate and local woods. • His dad had recently bought a new drill and saw. • Father and son (accompanied by Jim's mother and the dog) headed towards the bottom of the garden.
42.	Up to 2	*Award **2 marks** to pupils who correctly state '**Jim's Tree House**' is a **fictional** text written in the **third person**. This is evidenced by the writer using informal language and is focussed on helping us to understand Jim and his ideas. For the full **2 marks**, pupils also need to quote **two** examples from the text.* Examples: • Jim was extremely passionate about one thing and one thing only: tree houses. • He wanted to design a modern tree house. • Jim had his heart set on using the large oak tree. • "The post method?!" He whined. "That's so boring! It has to be suspended, all my designs and drawings are based on a suspended tree house." *Award **1 mark** if the pupil neglects to give any examples but correctly states 'Jim's Tree House' is a fictional text written in the third person.*

Exam.Ninja

© Exam Ninja

English Reading - Set B - Penguins

Q	Mark	Answers
1.	1	• Torpedo-shaped bodies. • Flipper like wing bones. • Great swimmers. *Award **1 mark** to pupils who state **any two** of the above.*
2.	1	Macaroni penguin — it's name. *Award **1 mark** if the answer **clearly indicates** that the macaroni penguin's crest of yellow feathers on its head looks like an 18th century macaroni hat.*
3.	1	*Award **1 mark** to pupils who **explain** it can't be true because Galapagos penguins come from tropical islands near the equator.*
4.	1	Rookeries.
5.	1	*Award **1 mark** to pupils who **explain** that penguins' behaviour of feeding, swimming and nesting in groups suggests that they are social creatures.*
6.	1	*Award **1 mark** to pupils who have clearly identified that larger penguins would have extra body mass and fat to help protect them from the cold climate.*
7.	Up to 2	*Award **1 mark** to pupils who **explain** that camouflage is when animals can blend into their surroundings, making it harder for predators to spot them. An acceptable alternative explanation would be that when camouflaged, animals are not easily spotted as their colour matches the surroundings.*
8.	1	7
9.	1	*Award **1 mark** to pupils who correctly identify them as all having bright yellow feathers on their heads that look like eyebrows.*
10.	1	Staple diet.
11.	1	*Award **1 mark** to pupils who **explain** that a '**distinct call**' means that each penguin makes a different sound or individual noise (accept a similar explanation). An acceptable alternative explanation would be that penguins can tell each call apart.*
12.	Up to 2	*Award **2 marks** to pupils who correctly identify the text as being **factual** and that its purpose is to **give its readers information about penguins.** Incorrect answer? Award **1 mark** if a pupil has stated that it's a factual text **or** that its purpose is to give its readers information about penguins.*

Q	Mark	Answers
13.	**1**	Award **1 mark** to pupils who describe a storm, stormy weather, strong winds, heavy rain *(accept a similar explanation)*.
14.	**Up to 2**	Award **2 marks** to pupils who explain his face feels '**numb**' and '**raw**' from the cold weather and/or strong wind. For the full **2 marks**, pupils also **need** to quote **one** example from the text. Examples: '**stinging insects**' or '**howling gusts**'. Award **1 mark** to pupils who correctly **explain** his face feels numb and raw from the cold weather and/or strong wind but neglect to include a suitable example from the text.
15.	**1**	The **second** option: It was so windy he could hardly stand up.
16.	**1**	Award **1 mark** to pupils who describe a strong gust of wind pushing him to the ground *(accept a similar explanation)*.
17.	**Up to 2**	• Grimaced • Promised • Shrieked Award **2 marks** to pupils who list **all three** of the words. Incorrect answer? Award **1 mark** to pupils that correctly list **two** of the three words.
18.	**Up to 2**	Award **2 marks** to pupils who demonstrate an understanding that the author is using the phrases to suggest the house is alive, has feelings or is like a person *(accept a similar explanation)*.
19.	**Up to 2**	Award **1 mark** to pupils who describe Henry as feeling **scared, frightened** or **anxious** *(accept a similar explanation)* about going into the house. Award a further **1 mark** for pupils who quote 'It looks like something out of a horror film'.
20.	**1**	• Yanked frantically • Stubborn doors Award **1 mark** to pupils who state **either** of the phrases above.
21.	**1**	The staircase.
22.	**1**	The wind, storm, stormy weather, strong winds, heavy rain outside *(accept a similar explanation)*.

© Exam Ninja

Q	Mark	Answers
23.	1	*Award **1 mark** to pupils who explain that the author wants to create suspense (accept a similar explanation).* *A suitable alternative answer could be that the author's ending (using ellipses) encourages readers to read on so we find out what happens next.*
24.	Up to 2	*Award **2 marks** to pupils who explain that '**Raven Hall**' is a fictional story and go on to say that it uses detailed descriptions and/or speech to help us understand the atmosphere and the characters (accept similar answers). For the full **2 marks**, pupils also **need** to quote **two** examples from the text.* Examples: • I could hardly see the path in front of me as I braced against the howling gusts. • The storm was now so violent that we'd have settled for anywhere that was remotely dry. • "Oh dear, it's like something out of a horror film," • "I'm going in," I shrieked as I yanked frantically on the stubborn doors of Old Raven. • "That's strange," mumbled Henry. *Incorrect answer? Award **1 mark** to pupils who correctly state '**Raven Hall**' is a fictional story (and go on to give two supporting examples) but neglect to **explain** how it is fictional.*

English Reading - Set B - Witches

Q	Mark	Answers
25.	1	*The **third** option:* Roman Law celebrated good magic and punished you for harmful magic.
26.	Up to 2	• Harm • Accidents • Illnesses • Bad Luck • Death *Award **2 marks** for pupils who correctly state any **four** of the above.* *Incorrect answer? Award **1 mark** if a pupil states any **two** of the above.*
27.	1	Heresy.
28.	1	1230 AD.

Q	Mark	Answers
29.	Up to 2	*Award **2 marks** to pupils who state that the author doesn't dislike witches but is instead telling us what other people thought at the time. For the full **2 marks**, pupils also **need** to quote **two** examples from the text.* Examples: • They believed that witches could cause accidents. • Historically, people have associated witchcraft with evil.
30.	1	The grip of freezing weather during the late 1500s and early 1600s.
31.	Up to 2	• Imprisonment (accept put in prison). • Banished. • Execution (accept drowning in river). *Award **2 marks** for pupils that correctly state **any three** of the above.* *Incorrect answer? Award **1 mark** if a pupil states **any two** of the above.*
32.	1	*Award **1 mark** to pupils that explain that people were not given a fair trial because if they survived the test then they were killed anyway (accept a similar explanation).*
33.	1	1951.
34.	1	*Award **1 mark** to pupils who state it went '**underground**' because it was made illegal.*
35.	Up to 2	*Award **2 marks** to pupils that clearly explain that nobody would want to use magic to harm anyone because (according to the Threefold Law of Karma) it would only return to them three times worse (accept a similar explanation).*
36.	Up to 2	*Award **2 marks** to pupils who explain that '**Witches**' is a **factual** text that uses historical information to help readers understand the history of witches (accept a similar explanation). For the full **2 marks** pupils also need to give **two** examples from the text to support their answer.* Examples: • The Inquisition, which began about 1230 AD, was an effort by the church to seek. • out and punish heretics and force them to change their beliefs. • The witch-hunt reached its peak in Europe during the late 1500s and early 1600s.

Exam Ninja

© Exam Ninja

Q	Mark	Answers
37.	Up to 2	Award **2 marks** to pupils who clearly **explain** that the author feels sad or sorry for witches (accept a similar explanation). Pupils may mention that the author writes about... • 'Gruesome Facts' so readers can try to understand and sympathise with how difficult life must have been during witch-hunts. • How modern witches practise their religion today, to help readers further understand them rather than fear them. For the full **2 marks** pupils also **need** to give **two** examples from the text to support their answer. Examples: • Most historians doubt that worship of the Devil was ever widespread, if indeed it even took place, but stories about it created a mood of fear and anxiety. • Either way, you were not given a fair trial! • Witches also believe in the Threefold Law of Karma, which says that magic returns to the sender, magnified three times.

English Reading - Set C - Know Your Trees

Q	Mark	Answers
1.	1	The English oak — is the third most common tree in Britain. The yew tree — produces acorns when it is at least 40 years old. The ash tree — is an evergreen conifer.
2.	1	Award **1 mark** to pupils that describe that the words '**ever**' and '**green**' imply that the trees are always green or forever green (accept a similar explanation).
3.	1	Deciduous.
4.	1	The yew tree.
5.	Up to 2	False, True, False, True. Award **2 marks** for correctly answering the question. Incorrect answer? Award **1 mark** if there are **two** or more correct answers.
6.	Up to 2	Award **2 marks** to pupils who explain native as meaning where something originally came from or where it was first found (accept a similar explanation).
7.	1	In a churchyard or among hedging.

Q	Mark	Answers
8.	1	**Red, fleshy** and **berry-like**. *Award **1 mark** to pupils that list **all** of the above.*
9.	1	*Award **1 mark** to pupils who identify the outer seed coat as being toxic (or poisonous).*
10.	1	Dioecious.
11.	1	*Award **1 mark** to pupils who describe the author's reasons as being either to emphasise its importance or to draw a reader's attention to it (accept a similar explanation).*
12.	1	*The **third** option:* The airy canopy and early leaf fall allow sunlight to reach the floor.
13.	Up to 2	*Award **2 marks** to pupils who explain that writing in the third person allows the author to sound more knowledgeable, objective or write more easily without bias. For the full **2 marks**, pupils also **need** to quote **two** examples from the text.* Examples: • The foliage and seed coat of a yew tree is highly toxic. • The yew is an evergreen conifer native to the UK, Europe and North Africa. • Ash trees make the perfect habitat for a number of different species of wildlife.

English Reading - Set C - The River Whale

Q	Mark	Answers
14.	1	It was Jack's birthday.
15.	1	*Award **1 mark** to pupils who describe the people as looking small on London bridge because they were far away.*
16.	1	St Paul's Cathedral.
17.	Up to 2	*Award **1 mark** to pupils who describe the people as feeling amazed or excited (accept a similar explanation).* *Award a further **1 mark** to pupils who correctly identify '**rushed gleefully**' as the words that support this.*
18.	1	There was blood in the water.

Exam Ninja

© Exam Ninja

Q	Mark	Answers
19.	1	Award **1 mark** to pupils who explain that the boat was badly damaged (accept a similar explanation).
20.	1	The **first** option: Encourage.
21.	1	Award **1 mark** to pupils who explain that the helicopter was 'filming', 'recording for the TV' or 'broadcasting' (or similar words and phrases).
22.	1	The **third** option: Because it was too hot outside.
23.	Up to 2	Award **2 marks** to pupils who explain that the whale was clearly in a great deal of pain, badly cut, distressed (accept a similar explanation).
24.	Up to 2	When they're ill and when they have damage to their hearing. Award **1 mark** for **each** correct answer.
25.	1	It was the first record of a **bottle nosed whale** found in the river since records began (accept that a bottle nosed whale had never been found in the river before and similar explanations).
26.	Up to 2	Award **2 marks** to pupils who explain that writing in the third person allows the author to easily swap from one character's viewpoint to another as well as adding their own opinions. Further to this it allows the author to describe action happening in different places at the same time as well as giving extra facts or information. For the full **2 marks**, pupils also **need** to quote **one** example from the text. Examples: • Everybody rushed gleefully to the sides to catch a glimpse but it was soon clear that the creature was no dolphin. • He pulled out his camera and took a picture. • Arjun didn't believe it. • Jack's mum called the police. • The plan was to keep it away from the banks, guide it down the river, and out to sea. • Apparently it was the first record of a bottle nosed whale found in the Thames since records began.

Q	Mark	Answers
27.	Up to 2	Award pupils **2 marks** for stating **two** of the facts from the text and going on to explain that whilst the author is clearly telling a story, they have included facts to inform (accept 'teach' or similar words) readers about whales. Examples: • "But those whales live miles away in the deep seas of the North Atlantic." • Sometimes whales can get lost or beached when they're ill, or sometimes they have hearing damage which can make them confused.

English Reading - Set C - Super Storm Sandy

Q	Mark	Answers
28.	1	• East Coast US • Atlantic City • Manhattan • New York • New Jersey (accept New Jersey Coast) • Queens • Ocean City *Award **1 mark** to pupils that list any **three** of the above.*
29.	1	5.2 million (or 5,200,000).
30.	1	Award **1 mark** to pupils who have described '**evacuate**' to mean '**had to leave**', '**forced to leave**' (accept a similar explanation).
31.	1	• 'Super storm' • 'carved a path of destruction' • 'ripping up' • 'sending cars floating' • 'damaging' • 'menace' • 'trail of death' *Award **1 mark** to pupils that list any **two** of the above.*
32.	1	Blaze.

Exam Ninja

© Exam Ninja

Q	Mark	Answers
33.	Up to 2	*Award* **1 mark** *to pupils who quote the following sentence:* *'A record breaking 13-foot surge of seawater hit New York City and flooded the Brooklyn-Battery tunnel, a major traffic route.'* *Award another* **1 mark** *to pupils who then explain that parts of New York's subway had stopped working and would remain closed for at least a week.*
34.	1	90mph.
35.	1	An historic pier.
36.	1	*Award* **1 mark** *to pupils who explain that by comparing the number of children to the population of Norway, the author is trying to help the reader understand that it's an enormous number (accept a similar explanation).*
37.	1	*Award* **1 mark** *to pupils who explain Mrs Franchock's house was now flooded and without electricity.*
38.	Up to 2	*Award* **2 marks** *to pupils who explain that 'Super Storm Sandy Strikes U.S.' is a factual news report, written to inform readers about the progression of the storm. It uses powerful, descriptive language to tell readers how the storm has affected the people and the landscape.* Examples: • Super storm Sandy carved a path of destruction through the East Coast on Monday, ripping up Atlantic City and sending cars floating through the streets of Manhattan in New York. • The impact was mounting. As night fell on Monday, a record breaking 13-foot surge of seawater hit New York City. • Over the course of the day, as winds strengthened to 90 miles per hour. • The storm left a trail of death. *Only award* **1 mark** *if the pupil simply states that it's a factual text (with suitable examples) and* **neglects to explain** *how they know this.*
39.	Up to 2	*Award* **1 mark** *to pupils who explain that the people did not take the warnings seriously and were unaware of the real dangers. They carried on with their everyday activities such as walking their dogs and drinking their coffee as though it were entertainment or a local attraction.* *Award a further* **1 mark** *to pupils who describe the author's use of 'gawk' is to imply the stupidity (accept a similar explanation) of the people to put themselves in such direct danger.*

KEY STAGE 2
GRAMMAR, PUNCTUATION AND SPELLING

ANSWERS & MARK SCHEMES

© Exam Ninja

About the Grammar, Punctuation and Spelling Practice Papers

There are three **full** sets of **KS2 Grammar, Punctuation and Spelling Practice Papers.**

Each set of KS2 Grammar, Punctuation and Spelling Practice Papers consists of two separate tasks: Paper 1 **(Questions)** and Paper 2 **(Spelling)**.

 This pencil sign means that an answer needs to be written either where indicated by the pencil or in the position instructed in the question.

Paper 1 (Questions)

Paper 1 of the Grammar, Punctuation and Spelling Test is the Questions task. This lasts for **45 minutes** and has a total of **50 marks**.

Paper 2 (Spelling)

Paper 2 is the Spelling Task, an **audible test**. This lasts for approximately **20 minutes** and has a total of **20 marks**. For information about how to administer the Spelling Task including the instructions, transcripts and where to download the **FREE** audio, see page **73**.

Marking and Assessing the Papers

Once your child has completed a test, mark it using the **Answers and Mark Scheme** within this book. Note: in order to mark **Paper 2 (Spelling)**, use the transcripts on page **73**.

Add up the marks and write them in the table below. After completing a full set of papers, add up the scores for Paper 1 (Questions) and Paper 2 (Spelling) to get a total out of **70**.

Grammar, Punctuation and Spelling Marks Table

	SET A	SET B	SET C
Paper 1 (Questions) (45 mins, out of 50)			
Paper 2 (Spelling) (20 mins, out of 20)			
Total (out of 70)			

Grammar, Punctuation & Spelling - Paper 1 (Questions) Set A Answers

Q	Mark	Answers
1.	1	The old (dog) sat on his favourite (cushion) next to the (fire.)
2.	1	**We**'re going to **J**ulia's party on **S**aturday.
3.	1	The **fourth** option: Quietly
4.	Up to 2	Ladies, mice. Match, baby. *Award **2 marks** to pupils who correctly answered the question.* *Incorrect answer? Award **1 mark** if there are **two** correct answers.*
5.	1	How do you tie a knot**?** First you make a loop**.** Quick, he has tripped on his laces**!** *Award **2 marks** for the correct answer.*
6.	1	Jack said that he was going for a swim because it was too hot in the sun. *Award **1 mark** for a similar indirect sentence.*
7.	Up to 2	Conceal – Cover Quarrel – Argue Shift – Move Anxious – Worried *Award **2 marks** for correctly answering the question.* *Incorrect answer? Award **1 mark** if there are **two** correct links.*
8.	Up to 2	Couldn't, I'll, can't, we'll *Award **2 marks** for correctly answering the question.* *Incorrect answer? Award **1 mark** if there are **two** correct answers.*
9.	Up to 2	Unarmed, incurable, disadvantaged *Award **2 marks** for the correct answer.*
10.	Up to 2	go is were *Award **2 marks** for the correct answer.* *Incorrect answer? Award **1 mark** to pupils that correct **two** of the grammatical mistakes.*

Exam Ninja

© Exam Ninja

Q	Mark	Answers
11.	1	There were roses, daffodils, giant daisies and foxgloves in the garden.
12.	1	*The **fourth** option:* To separate items in a list.
13.	1	The (rusty-red) leaves of the (ancient) tree, fluttered in the (warm) breeze.
14.	1	*Jack's father (whose full name was Louis Penrose) mainly farmed vegetables, whole grains, fruit and herbs.*
15.	1	He, him, she
16.	Up to 2	Jacob's, dogs' *Award **2 marks** to pupils who correctly answered the question.* *Incorrect answer? Award **1 mark** if a pupil gave **one** correct answer.*
17.	1	*Inside the cave* ☐ *the ground was laden with jewels* ☑ *rubies, emeralds, opals, ☐ sapphires and hundreds of diamonds!*
18.	1	*The **third** option:* "Oh no, what time is it?" asked Dan. "We're going to be late if we don't hurry up."
19.	1	*Patrick wants to build <u>a</u> robot using his new robotics kit, but he can't find <u>any</u> batteries in <u>the</u> box!*
20.	1	*Can you hold my dog for <u>me</u> while <u>I</u> go into the shop?* *Janet asked if <u>I</u> had seen her cat.* *My mum helped <u>me</u> build my volcano project.*
21.	1	Brackets
22.	1	*The **third** option:* There are over 170 billion galaxies in the universe, ours is called the Milky Way.
23.	1	*They had a brilliant picnic <u>despite</u> the rain.* *I held the sail to stop it from flapping <u>while</u> Jane grappled with the ropes.* *I had eaten all of my dinner <u>but</u> there was still room for pudding.*

Q	Mark	Answers
24.	1	Descend - Ascend Interior - Exterior Hinder - Help Feast - Famine
25.	1	Najima was a girl (who / which) loved to dance. The television, (who / which) was ten years old, was taken to the charity shop. We had a cat (who / which) used to love sitting in the window.
26.	1	We're nearly there; it's just behind that building. Jack could just about squeeze between the two boulders and was finally free.
27.	Up to 2	The **first**, **second** and **fifth** options: It is written in the present tense. It uses commas to separate clauses. It uses prepositions to order the text. Award **2 marks** for the correct answer. Incorrect answer? Award **1 mark** to pupils that have only made **one** mistake (e.g. ticked an extra statement or incorrectly ticked a further statement). **Do not** award any marks to pupils that have ticked all the statements.
28.	Up to 2	<table><tr><th></th><th>Noun</th><th>Verb</th></tr><tr><td>panicked</td><td></td><td>✔</td></tr><tr><td>room</td><td>✔</td><td></td></tr><tr><td>fear</td><td>✔</td><td></td></tr><tr><td>experienced</td><td></td><td>✔</td></tr><tr><td>earthquake</td><td>✔</td><td></td></tr><tr><td>knew</td><td></td><td>✔</td></tr></table> Award **2 marks** to pupils who correctly answered the question. Incorrect answer? Award **1 mark** if there are **four** correct answers.
29.	1	The **first** and the **third** options: Shall we go to the zoo Where is the lion enclosure

Q	Mark	Answers		
30.	Up to 2		**Phrase**	**Clause**
		I can't see anything in this fog.		✔
		The trees were quite damaged **since the storm in November.**	✔	
		The acrobats were incredible **in the circus show.**	✔	
		Squirrels love to jump *from tree to tree.*		✔

*Award **2 marks** to pupils who correctly answered the question.*
*Incorrect answer? Award **1 mark** if there are **two** correct answers.*

Q	Mark	Answers
31.	1	Yesterday I <u>went</u> to the cinema with my best friend. She wanted to <u>go</u> to the sweet shop first. I said we were <u>going</u> to be late if we did.
32.	1	*The **second** option:* It felt like we were flying for a few magnificent moments.
33.	Up to 2	*The tiny fish swam frantically.* ↑ ↑ ↑ ↑ C A B D *Award **2 marks** for the correct answer.* *Incorrect answer? Award **1 mark** to pupils that have correctly placed **two** letters.*
34.	1	*The **fourth** option:* Chose

Q	Mark	Answers

35. | Up to 2 |

Sentence	Subordinating conjunction	Preposition
Can you pick up the kids <u>after</u> swimming?		✔
Shall we go shopping <u>after</u> we leave the leisure centre?	✔	
The shopping centre stays open <u>until</u> 10pm.		✔
Dad can pick us up <u>since</u> he no longer has to go to work.	✔	

*Award **2 marks** to pupils who correctly answered the question.*
*Incorrect answer? Award **1 mark** if there are **two** correct answers.*

---

36. | 1 | ⓙeevan was excited because it was finally ⓜonday the 1st ⓙanuary and he was visiting ⓘndia for the first time.

---

37. | 1 | Maria went to (she / ⓗer) meeting in a bad mood.
(Ⓣhey / Them) decided to go by car.
He parked the car next to (ⓗis / him) house.

---

38. | 1 | After their exhausting race, the rowers were all sleeping.

---

39. | 1 | *Amazingly,* whales are the descendants of land dwelling mammals, *first taking to the sea around 50 million years ago.*

Exam Ninja

© Exam Ninja

Grammar, Punctuation & Spelling - Paper 1 (Questions) Set B Answers

Q	Mark	Answers
1.	1	Can you see that**?** Wow, it's a shooting star**!** I was looking the other way**.**

2. | Up to 2 |

Word	Noun	Adjective	Verb	Adverb
young		✔		
cat	✔			
pounced			✔	
joyfully				✔

*Award **2 marks** to pupils who correctly answered the question.*
*Incorrect answer? **Award 1** mark if there are **two** correct answers.*

Q	Mark	Answers
3.	1	The crisps were finished by Henry.
4.	1	Alfie grabbed his new comics and hid in the small cupboard. There was no way that Mum was going to take his <u>fantastic Secret Soldier comic books</u> away from him!
5.	1	He <u>**went**</u> to the cinema yesterday. They <u>**go**</u> every year. She will <u>**be**</u> late as usual. I'll <u>**give**</u> him the last piece of cake.
6.	1	*"You should never climb without a rope, warned Frank.* ↑ ✔
7.	1	*The **first** and **fourth** options:* I can't play the piano very well. Our neighbours are in a band.
8.	1	After seeing their exam results, the children were extremely pleased.

Q	Mark	Answers
9.	Up to 2	(It's) dogs like (Jenny's) that scare me, (they're) too big and energetic. *Award 1 mark for correctly circling all the words that require apostrophes.* It's – to show letter omission. Jenny's – to show possession. They're – to show letter omission. *Award 1 mark for correctly explaining any of the above reasons.*
10.	Up to 2	One fly, several <u>flies</u>. One <u>pony</u>, four ponies. One match, a box of <u>matches</u>. One sheep, a herd of <u>sheep</u>. *Award 2 marks to pupils who correctly answered the question.* *Incorrect answer? Award 1 mark if there are two correct answers.*
11.	1	Bear
12.	1	The (mysterious) (wooden) chest popped open to reveal (brilliant) diamonds!
13.	1	

Word	Verb	Adjective
Dodge	✔	
Quick		✔
Went	✔	
Graceful		✔

Q	Mark	Answers
14.	1	We skipped (happily) towards the beach but were (suddenly) stopped by a parade marching (loudly).
15.	1	*The **first** option:* Corrina packed her jumper, hat and gloves.
16.	1	Josh has not got any more chances to get in the team now! *(Accept similar Standard English answers).*
17.	1	She'll (perform)/ performs) to the judges tomorrow. Rosie (have /(has)) a terrible cold. My aunty is a singing teacher who (train /(trains)) opera singers.
18.	1	*The **third** option:* They, their, they

Exam Ninja

© Exam Ninja

Q	Mark	Answers
19.	1	I like going in the sea (despite) my fear of sharks.
20.	1	*The **second** option:* On the way to Cornwall I saw many sheep.
21.	1	He (shouted) at the puzzle angrily and (stormed) upstairs.
22.	1	*<u>She</u> had defeated the mighty dragon.* *It had taken all of <u>her</u> strength.* *The dragon called Freda was now gone and <u>she</u> would never return.*
23.	Up to 2	Re ⟍ understanding Over ⟍⟋ marine Im ⤬ consider Sub ⤬ cook Mis ⟋ possible *Award **2 marks** for the correct answer.* *Incorrect answer? Award **1 mark** if there are **three** correct links.*
24.	1	*The **second** option:* The house was very old she lived with her cat.
25.	1	While in his rocket in space, Daniel <u>hobbs</u> counted down the days till <u>christmas</u>. The 25th <u>december</u> was a special day; not just because it was Christmas but because he was coming home to <u>earth</u>.
26.	1	Jake, who looks after elephants, has fed Jojo, Sila and Naj this morning.
27.	1	• Unhappy • Unimportant • Misinform • Disapprove
28.	1	*The children moved (**carefully, nervously, steadily, slowly**) across the ledge.* *It was dangerous but once on the other side they could run around* *(**freely, excitedly, joyfully**).* *Accept other suitable adverbs.*

Q	Mark	Answers
29.	1	*The **first** option:* baking
30.	Up to 2	I used a **saw** to cut some wood. I **saw** a bird in the sky yesterday. *Award **2 marks** to pupils whose answer clearly uses the word 'saw' with the same meaning as both of the examples above.* *Incorrect answer? Award **1 mark** to pupils that use the word 'saw' with the same meaning as one of the examples above.*
31.	1	• lived • let • thumped
32.	1	*The **second** option:* Calm, relaxed.
33.	1	⌢The⌣ sofa was ripped to shreds. I love ⌢a⌣ long walk. There's ⌢an⌣ egg in its nest.

34. Up to 2

Sentence	Subordinating conjunction	Coordinating conjunction
Janet couldn't pick up Hugh after swimming <u>because</u> her car was stuck in the garage.	✔	
My sister Daisy has too many toys <u>and</u> too many clothes.		✔
It's essential to wait <u>until</u> the water has started to boil.	✔	
While Susan's at work, her dog Bret sleeps on the bed, <u>and</u> her cat Floyd sleeps in the sink!		✔

*Award **2 marks** to pupils who correctly answered the question.*
*Incorrect answer? Award **1 mark** if there are **two** correct answers.*

Exam Ninja

© Exam Ninja

Q	Mark	Answers
35.	1	Jack <u>finished</u> his project <u>hastily</u> and went to watch the <u>live</u> band. A ↑ B ↑ D ↑ C ↑

35. Jack <u>finished</u> his project <u>hastily</u> and went to watch the <u>live</u> band.

↑   ↑   ↑   ↑

A   B   D   C

36. Mark: 1

Sentence	Omission	Possession
Annika's hamster is called Hammy.		✔
We'll never let them cut down our tree!	✔	
He couldn't see the road for the fog.	✔	

37. Mark: 1

- I'd
- don't

38. Mark: Up to 2

Sentence	Main Clause	Subordinate Clause
I baked a cake for the party **but it melted in the car**		✔
The birds flew high above the corn fields, searching for their prey.	✔	
If you look hard enough, you can see the North Star.		✔
Four ice creams later and **Johanna was feeling sick.**	✔	

Award **2 marks** for the correct answer.

Incorrect answer? Award **1 mark** if there are **two** correctly ticked boxes.

Q	Mark	Answers
39.	1	I was proud to reach the top it <u>although</u> was hard work. We left a flag on the mountain <u>so</u> other people could see we had made it. I don't think I'll do it again <u>because</u> I'm getting old!
40.	1	The **third** option: I watched patiently as he prepared my meal.

41.   Up to 2

Sentence	Phrase	Clause
Sally bought some **new ballet shoes.**		✔
He lost his wallet on the train.	✔	
The paper plane floated down **from the window.**		✔
Fluffy likes to sleep on Janet's lap.	✔	

Award **2 marks** to pupils who correctly answered the question.
Incorrect answer? Award **1 mark** if there are **two** correct answers.

Q	Mark	Answers
42.	1	The **third** option: Anna (my best friend) has gone on holiday.

Exam Ninja

© Exam Ninja

Grammar, Punctuation & Spelling - Paper 1 (Questions) Set C Answers

Q	Mark	Answers
1.	1	

Word	Adjective	Verb
thought		✔
brilliant	✔	
knew		✔
clever	✔	

Q	Mark	Answers
2.	Up to 2	*One door, three <u>doors</u>.* *One knife, two <u>knives</u>.* *One <u>puppy</u>, a litter of puppies.* *One fish, a shoal of <u>fish</u>.* *Award **2 marks** for all **four** correct answers.* *Incorrect answer? Award **1 mark** if there are **two** correct answers.*
3.	1	The waves in Cornwall are great for surfing**.** Look out it's a shark**!** Where is the ice-cream hut**?**
4.	1	Bow
5.	1	All the fish <u>were</u> swimming in the water. I <u>go</u> to the cinema every Friday. They <u>did</u> their homework on the bus! Fido <u>was</u> an obedient dog.
6.	1	*The soldiers all returned from the training field.(They) had built quite an appetite and the food that was put out for (them) looked magnificent. All of (them) were grateful for such a tasty treat, especially Captain Rogerson!*
7.	1	Peter Lions drove the school bus.
8.	1	Pleased (or any other suitable synonym).

Q	Mark	Answers
9.	1	*"Wait, wait wait "* screamed Karen as she ran after the bus.

Q	Mark	Answers
10.	1	After the match, everyone in the football team showered.
11.	1	Wash your hands.
12.	1	*Last (wednesday,)(june 22nd,)(juliette) went on holiday with her best friends (martha) and (fatima.)* Award **1 mark** for circling **all** of the correct words.
13.	1	Shall we ((eat)/ eaten) after the film? Bonso often (forget /(forgets)) he's a just a dog They rarely (goes /(go)) swimming.
14.	1	Award **1 mark** for any suitable adjective. Examples include (but are not limited to): Fred, who loves boats took his (**red, small, favourite**) rowing boat on the (**clear, calm, blue**) water.
15.	1	To make (jam,) all you do is boil (fruit) with (sugar) and (water)
16.	1	The wolves were howling (mournfully) while the hunters walked (cautiously) over the icy lake.
17.	1	The **first** and **fifth** options: Concentrate on the problem. Call 999!
18.	1	(see table below)

Word	Noun	Adverb
Donkey	✔	
Cleverly		✔
Perfectly		✔
Daisy	✔	

Exam.Ninja

© Exam Ninja

Q	Mark	Answers
19.	1	(Although) we were tired, we managed to finish the task.
20.	1	The **second**, **third** and **fourth** options: Do you want any more of those sweets? Amy liked her mobile phone more than Rhiannon's. Philip paid £2 more for his ticket than Peter did!

21. Up to 2

Sentence	Certainty	Possibility
Sorry Philip, I can't come to your party on Friday.	✔	
I may be able to give you a lift to school next week.		✔
We could have fish and chips for tea if you like?		✔
Alex will take the broken washing machine back later.	✔	

Award **2 marks** to pupils who correctly answer the question.
Incorrect answer? Award **1 mark** to pupils that correctly state **two** answers.

Q	Mark	Answers
22.	1	The **fourth** option: I, your
23.	1	The **second** option: Don't forget to tell: Mr Pollock, the milkman, the neighbours and of course, Jasmine.
24.	1	I ordered a coffee for you. Do you want me and Harry to give you a lift? George and I played in the sea all day.
25.	1	"What a load of nonsense," said the policeman who was shaking his head. "It couldn't be him as he was already in prison!"
26.	1	The **second** option: Simir held the kite while I untangled the knots.
27.	1	I can look after your hamster during your holiday abroad.

Q	Mark	Answers
28.	**1**	*They <u>take</u> the picture off the wall.* *They <u>see</u> the migrating birds from the plane.* *Jillian <u>collects</u> marbles, she had a special box for them.*
29.	**1**	*The dogs <u>couldn't</u> be trusted near the dinner table.* *Florence says <u>you're</u> supposed to wait here.*
30.	**Up to 2**	If I were you, I would not behave like that. Dad laughed and recommended that we use eggs the next time we try making pan-cakes. I suggest we head over to the beach tomorrow, it's due to be sunny. *(Accept similar verbs with suggestion or recommendation such as 'advise' or 'insist'.)* *Award **2 marks** to pupils that rewrite **all three sentences** in the subjunctive form **and** don't use the same verb more than once.* *Incorrect answer? Award **1 mark** to pupils that rewrite **two** sentences **and** use different verbs.*
31.	**Up to 2**	The mattress was too hard. The sums were too hard. *Award **2 marks** to pupils whose answer clearly uses the word 'hard' with the same meaning as **both** of the examples above.* *Incorrect answer? Award **1 mark** to pupils that use the word 'hard' with the same meaning as **one** of the examples above.*
32.	**1**	The dress is at the dry cleaners. She boiled an egg for lunch. I need to buy a new table.
33.	**1**	*The **first** option:* Some fish nibbled at our feet.
34.	**1**	<table><tr><th>Sentence</th><th>Omission</th><th>Possession</th></tr><tr><td>*The sheep's wool was soft.*</td><td></td><td>✔</td></tr><tr><td>*It's lamb chops for dinner.*</td><td>✔</td><td></td></tr><tr><td>*I'm a vegetarian.*</td><td>✔</td><td></td></tr></table>

Exam Ninja

© Exam Ninja

Q	Mark	Answers

35. Up to 2

Sentence	Phrase	Clause
The sun sets at 6:30pm.		✔
We don't have time **to stop for tea.**	✔	
Some cats are fierce **but some are friendly.**	✔	
Miranda fell into the nettles.		✔

*Award **2 marks** to pupils who correctly answer the question.*
*Incorrect answer? Award **1 mark** to pupils that correctly state **two** answers.*

36. Up to 2

Sentence	Progressive	Perfect
I was walking quickly until you came along!	✔	
Margaret and I have eaten all our lunch.		✔
Jason was thinking about going home soon.	✔	
We have lived in this house all our lives.		✔

*Award **2 marks** to pupils who correctly answer the question.*
*Incorrect answer? Award **1 mark** to pupils that correctly state **two** answers.*

37. Up to 2

Sentence	Main Clause	Subordinate Clause
Jay, **who never won anything**, collected first prize.		✔
They wanted cake when they could smell it.	✔	
Gavin, who was hungry, **ate everything in the fridge.**	✔	
She didn't go on the ride **because she was too scared.**		✔

Award **2 marks** to pupils who correctly answer the question.
Incorrect answer? Award **1 mark** to pupils that correctly state **two** answers.

38. 1 The **fourth** option:
Mr Lamb likes his wife's cooking Mrs Lamb hates his cooking.

39. 1 <u>Skilled</u> jugglers can <u>juggle</u> <u>effortlessly</u> with <u>bananas</u> and books.

       ↑   ↑   ↑   ↑

      C   B   D   A

40. 1 The **fourth** option:
The men's ties were all pink except one.

41. 1 James wanted to play computer games <u>after</u> dinner.
<u>Unfortunately</u> his wife still had work to do.
<u>So,</u> she asked him to wait <u>until</u> she had finished using the computer.

42. 1 The **fourth** option:
Sneakily

43. 1 When I travel the world (which I plan to do very soon) I will keep a diary (to help me remember my trip).

Exam.Ninja

© Exam Ninja

BLANK PAGE

KEY STAGE 2
GRAMMAR, PUNCTUATION AND SPELLING

SPELLING TRANSCRIPTS

© Exam Ninja

Using This Transcript

As part of buying this book you are entitled to download the audio for the **Spelling Papers** for **FREE** from:

http://www.ExamNinja.co.uk/audio

Simply go to the link and follow the instructions to download your audio.

We encourage you to use our recordings as they have been **professionally produced** to closely reflect those that children will face in the **real exam**. Simply play the relevant audio file and wait approximately 20 minutes until your child has finished the test.

In the event that you cannot use the audio files you should read aloud the following instructions:

- "Listen carefully to the instructions I am going to give you.

- I am going to read twenty sentences. Each sentence within your answer booklet has a word missing.

- You should listen carefully to the missing word and fill this in, making sure you spell it correctly.

- I will read the word, then the word within a sentence, then repeat the word a third time.

- You will not be able to ask questions once the test has begun so if you have any questions you may ask them now."

Answer any questions your child has. When they are ready to begin the test, tell them that you **will not** be able to answer **any** further questions or interrupt the test once you have started reading the questions.

The instructions and questions **must** be read out consistently. Start by stating the **question number** and **the word**, then **the word within a sentence** and finally **the word again**. Wait 10 seconds before asking the next question for your child to spell the word.

After the test has finished, remind children that they are **not allowed** to change their answers and that they should **remain seated** until their answer sheet has been collected.

Grammar, Punctuation & Spelling - Spelling Transcript : Set A

Q	Answers
1	*The word is: Appeared* *Suddenly, the dragon **appeared** from nowhere.*
2	*The word is: Reflect* *Julian attempted to **reflect** the rays of sunshine with his pocket mirror.*
3	*The word is: Dodge* *We had to **dodge** under the moving jib on the sailboat; otherwise we would have been knocked into the sea!*
4	*The word is: Snapped* *One of the crocodiles **snapped** angrily at the visitors.*
5	*The word is: Descend* *The brave window cleaner began to **descend** from the 50th floor of the building, hanging from a rope.*
6	*The word is: Relieved* *Once he was on the ground, he looked rather **relieved**.*
7	*The word is: Taught* *Children are **taught** that it is important to share with others.*
8	*The word is: Fought* *Two hippos violently **fought** over the territory.*
9	*The word is: Disgust* *She looked at the boy with utter **disgust** as he picked his nose.*
10	*The word is: Retrieve* *The police can train certain types of dogs to **retrieve** various illegal items.*
11	*The word is: Incredible* *The talented duo danced to an **incredible** standard and won the competition.*
12	*The word is: Journey* *It was a long and arduous **journey** from York to Kent.*
13	*The word is: Necessary* *It is **necessary** to have all the facts before making a legal decision.*

Exam.Ninja

© Exam Ninja

Q	Answers
14	*The word is: Doubt* *There is no **doubt** in my mind that you will have every success.*
15	*The word is: Whether* *It is not important **whether** it rains or not.*
16	*The word is: Recycle* *The neighbours **recycle** our food waste for us, as they have a garden with a compost heap.*
17	*The word is: Actually* *Global warming is **actually** changing the landscape of our planet.*
18	*The word is: Programmes* *You could watch many **programmes** on the subject of the environment and find that they all agree.*
19	*The word is: Dismantle* *Could you help me to **dismantle** this robot please?*
20	*The word is: Queue* *Outside the bank, there was a huge **queue** of angry customers.*

Q	Answers
1	*The word is: Slipped* *The comedian **slipped** on a banana skin.*
2	*The word is: Accident* *Mrs. Robbins was in a car **accident** and broke her arm.*
3	*The word is: Discussed* *The children **discussed** the topic of school uniforms at length.*
4	*The word is: Bicycle* *Someone stole my father's **bicycle**.*
5	*The word is: Assist* *I offered to **assist** the old lady to cross the road.*
6	*The word is: Disappear* *How could the keys just **disappear** like that?*
7	*The word is: Assemble* *On Saturday we will **assemble** the new bed.*
8	*The word is: Mysterious* *There was a **mysterious** knock at the door.*
9	*The word is: Lightning* *Thunder is the sound caused by **lightning**.*
10	*The word is: Anxious* *Martha was **anxious** about the spelling test.*
11	*The word is: Weather* *The **weather** was awful; it rained for the entire holiday.*
12	*The word is: Congratulations* ***Congratulations** on your engagement!*
13	*The word is: Ceremony* *The **ceremony** took place in a grand hall.*

© Exam Ninja

Q	Answers
14	*The word is: Cereal* My favourite **cereal** is porridge.
15	*The word is: Solution* If we keep trying, we will find a **solution**.
16	*The word is: Discovery* The scientist made a very important **discovery**.
17	*The word is: Quarrel* The children started to **quarrel** in the back of the car.
18	*The word is: Prepared* Mother **prepared** a picnic.
19	*The word is: Accidentally* I **accidentally** mixed the orange paint with blue and now it has turned a horrible brown colour!
20	*The word is: Serial* Almost everything in the shop has a **serial** number on the back.

Grammar, Punctuation & Spelling - Spelling Transcript : Set C

Q	Answers
1	*The word is: Afterwards.* *We can have some pudding **afterwards**.*
2	*The word is: Believe* *I don't **believe** in Father Christmas.*
3	*The word is: Capture* *They will **capture** you if they find you.*
4	*The word is: Capable* *I am perfectly **capable** of doing it on my own.*
5	*The word is: Cautious* *The cat was very **cautious** around the dog.*
6	*The word is: Disappoint* *I don't mean to **disappoint** you but there are no spaces left.*
7	*The word is: Disaster* *Japan suffered a major **disaster**.*
8	*The word is: Decide* *Poppy couldn't **decide** between the red or blue dress.*
9	*The word is: Decision* *Finally she made a **decision**.*
10	*The word is: Forgotten* *Has he completely **forgotten** his times tables?*
11	*The word is: Jealous* *The monkeys were **jealous** because the elephants had more peanuts.*
12	*The word is: Marvellous* *What a **marvellous** day for a picnic.*
13	*The word is: Notice* *The boy didn't even **notice** the big red letters on the warning sign.*

Exam Ninja

© Exam Ninja

Q	Answers
14	*The word is: Purpose* *Maybe he did it on **purpose**.*
15	*The word is: Immediately* *They came to the rescue **immediately**.*
16	*The word is: Regular* *I am a **regular** visitor at the museum.*
17	*The word is: Familiar* *This place looks **familiar**.*
18	*The word is: Similar* *Kate and Kelly have **similar** hair.*
19	*The word is: Suppose* *I don't **suppose** you could give me a lift?*
20	*The word is: Happened* *It all **happened** so quickly.*

NOTES

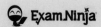

© Exam Ninja

NOTES

 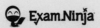

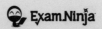

© Exam Ninja